This edition published in 2018 by Arcturus Publishing Limited
26/27 Bickels Yard, 151–153 Bermondsey Street,
London SE1 3HA

Copyright © Arcturus Holdings Limited

ISBN 978-1-78888-256-9
CH005906NT
Supplier 29, Date 0618, Print run 6463

Written by: William Potter
Illustrated by: Matthew Scott
Designed by: Well Nice
Edited by: Sebastian Rydberg

Printed in China

Dotty Doodle

Connect all the numbered dots that are part of the 3 times table. Start at 3 and go up to 36, then go back to 3 again. What shape does it make?

9
14
7
11
15
5
17
8
12
4
6
18
19
3
20
16
21
38
36
24
35
30
22
37
29
34
26
32
33
27

On the Trail

Help the hiker find his route by choosing the number path with the highest total. Choose any start and finish, but you cannot cross your path.

Finish

Finish

9

8

5

6

7   12

3

2

7

4

1

2

10

5

6

2

9

3

6

Start

Start

Start

Clever Clown

Fill in the missing numbers on each clown's juggling balls,
so that the equation gives the result on his nose.

Clown A — nose: 5

(-) ( ) ÷
3
x   2
5
4   =

Clown B — nose: 8

x   6
5   ÷
-    ( )
8
9   =

Clown C — nose: 18

÷   6
( )   x
+   9
18
7   =

Clown D — nose: 5

+   ( )
5   ÷
÷   3
5
20   =

Brick Build

Every brick in the pyramid shows a number equal to the two numbers on the bricks below it.

8

2   **6**

8 = 2 + 6

Which of the bricks along the bottom are needed to fill the gaps in the pyramid?

27

13   **11**   **15**

5   **3**   **9**

50	6	12	23	13
97	47	10	97	8
24	26	52	7	95

Cooking Costs

Find out how much each cooking ingredient costs by looking at the total price for each group.

9

11

14

13

2

Six Knights

Six castles have six knights. Fill in the empty squares with numbers 1 to 6. Each number must appear just once in each row, column, and block of six squares.

	6	1			4
	3		2	1	
1		4		3	
	2		4	6	1
6		2			
3			1		5

Out of Time

Clocks A and B were given the right time at
2 o'clock. Clock A goes fast and gains 5 minutes every hour.
Clock B is slow and loses 10 minutes every hour. What will
each clock say ...

... after three hours?

A   B

... after five hours?

A   B

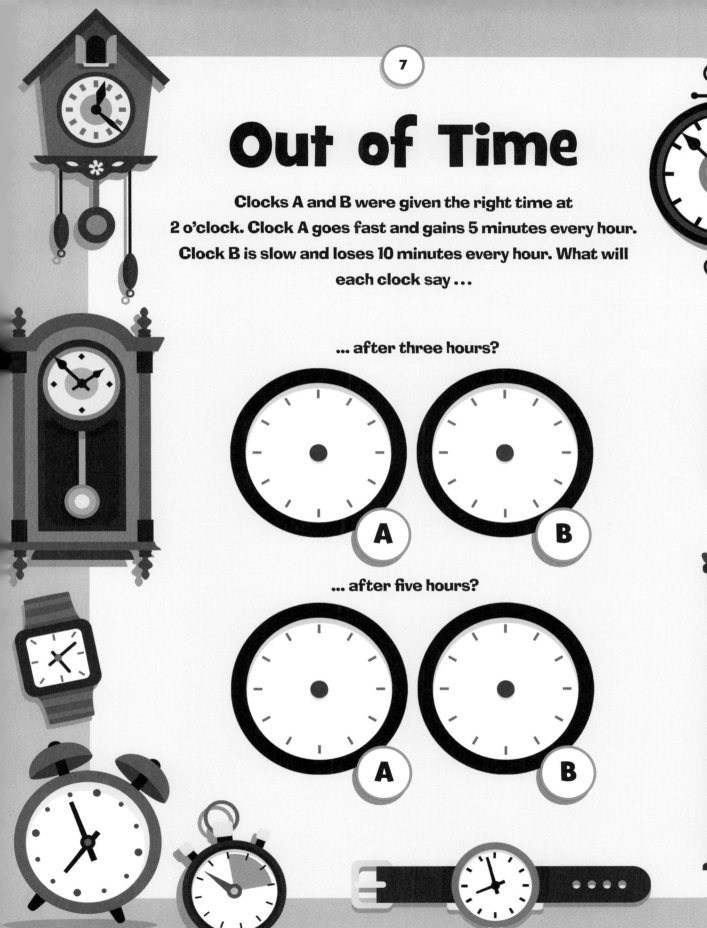

Mapmaker

Draw a line between all the coordinates on the map to reveal the shape of the castaway's island. The first line is done for you.

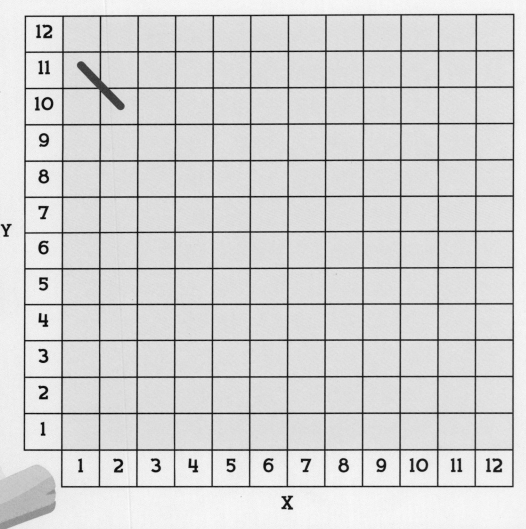

1,11; 2,10; 2,12; 3,10; 2,9; 3,7; 4,8; 4,11; 5,11; 5,8; 6,8; 6,11; 7,11; 7,8; 9,8; 10,9; 9,10; 10,12; 10,10; 11,12; 12,10; 11,9; 10,7; 10,6; 12,5; 10,5; 12,3; 10,4; 11,2; 10,3; 10,1; 9,3; 7,2; 5,3; 3,1; 4,3; 2,1; 3,3; 1,2; 2,4; 1,3; 2,5; 2,8; 1,9; 1,11

Pet Prizes

All these pets earned points for coming 1st, 2nd, and 3rd in their competitions. Look at the rosettes and cups next to each pet. Which won the most points?

1st 2nd 3rd

1st 2nd 3rd 3rd

2nd 3rd 2nd

1st 2nd

3rd 2nd 1st

3rd 1st

1st **25** 2nd **15** 3rd **5**

1st **40** 2nd **20** 3rd **10**

1st **30** 2nd **20** 3rd **10**

1st **15** 2nd **10** 3rd **5**

1st **50** 2nd **30** 3rd **10**

Pond Pals

Frog 3 can only step on lily pads with numbers in the 3 times table. Frog 4 can only follow the 4 times table. Which way should they go to reach the finish?

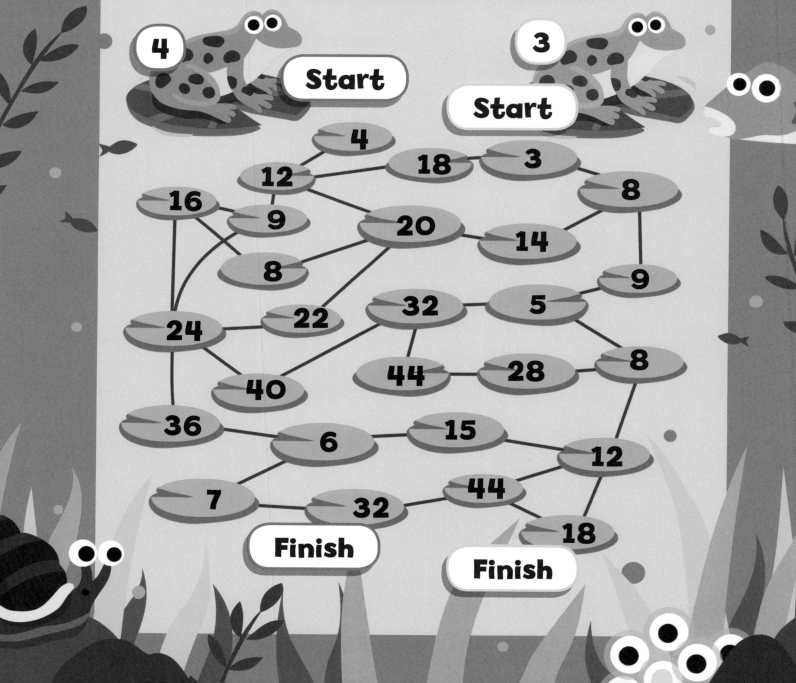

Number Bots

Each column in the robot display has a different effect on each start number: x 2, + 4, and so on. Fill in the missing results for the start numbers to the left of the box.

Start number	x 2	+ 4	x 3	- 7
10		14		
7				0
12			36	
20	40			

Dice Rolls

Three players took turns rolling dice to move along the board. Each player moved forward the number of squares shown at each roll of the die, following the arrows when they landed on them.
Look at the dice rolls. Who moved the farthest?

36	35	34	33	32	31
25	26	27	28	29	30
24	23	22	21	20	19
13	14	15	16	17	18
12	11	10	9	8	6
1	2	3	4	5	6

Sally   Jay   Angela

On Target

The archers have all fired five arrows, which are marked on the target by the small circles. Each band gives a different score. Who scored the most?

A

Dark blue arrows

15   10   5   2   1

B

Orange arrows

C

Light blue arrows

On the Scales

The scales are balanced to show that each side is the same weight. Calculate what each vegetable weighs on its own.

			2		

Chilly Challenge

Fill in the missing numbers on the Arctic ice floes.
The numbers in every row, column, and
diagonal should add up to 15.

4

1

8

Jolly Jewels

What comes next in each gem sequence?

A _____

B _____

C _____

D _____

Unicorn Style

Draw spots on 25% of the unicorns and stripes on a separate 25%. Then, draw stars on 50% of the ones remaining. If each unicorn only has one pattern, how many unicorns are left unpatterned?

Rocket Route

Which route through the asteroids should the astronaut take, so that the number on her suit becomes the number on her rocket?

Travel Saver

Ellie wants to travel from Home Town to Cheap City.
Look at the fares. Which is the cheapest route?
Hint: Ellie used more than one form of travel.

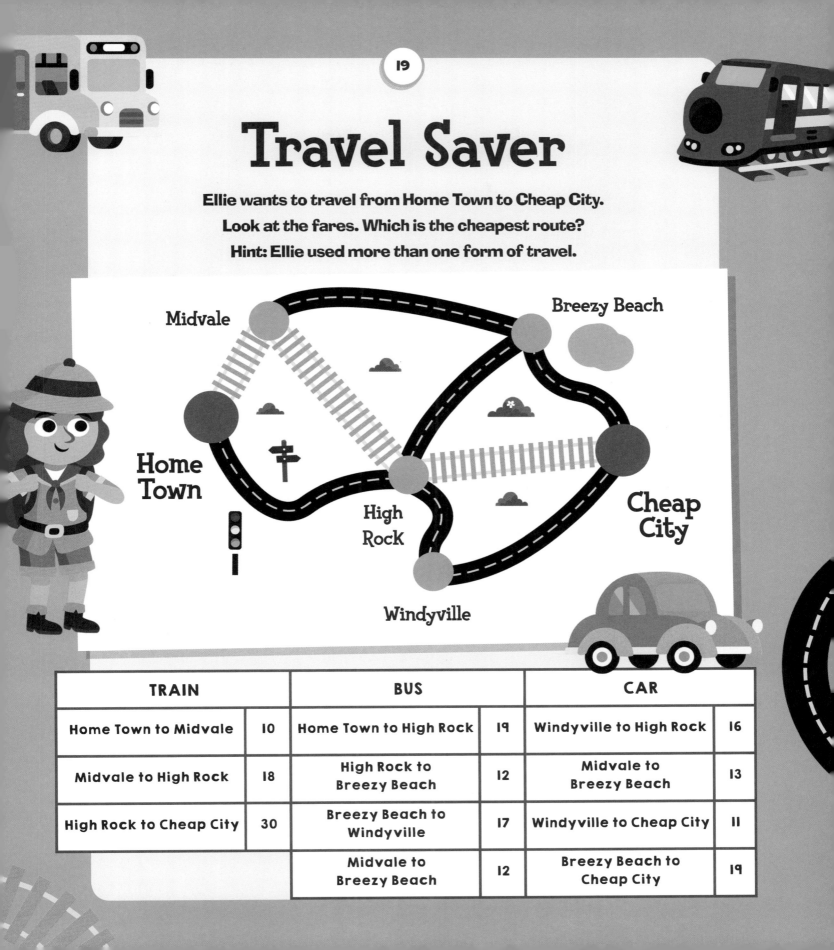

TRAIN		BUS		CAR	
Home Town to Midvale	10	Home Town to High Rock	19	Windyville to High Rock	16
Midvale to High Rock	18	High Rock to Breezy Beach	12	Midvale to Breezy Beach	13
High Rock to Cheap City	30	Breezy Beach to Windyville	17	Windyville to Cheap City	11
		Midvale to Breezy Beach	12	Breezy Beach to Cheap City	19

Superpowers

Fill in the missing numbers. The numbers 1 to 4 must appear once in every row and column in this grid. The arrows point from a square containing a higher number to a square containing a lower number.

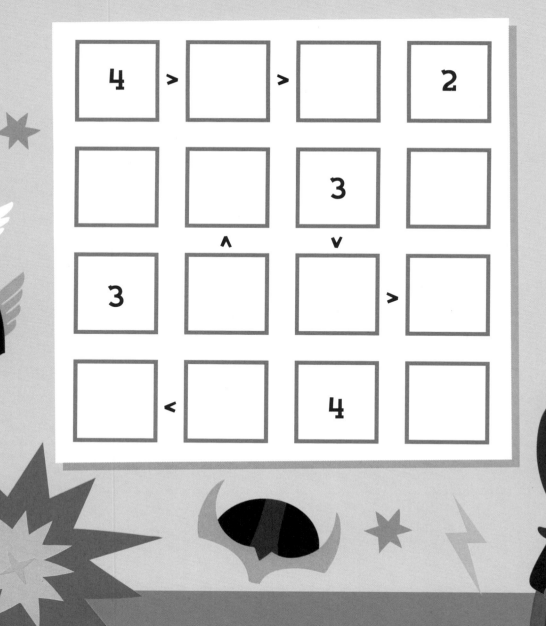

Egg Expert

If the rarest egg is worth 10, the second rarest worth 8, the third rarest 6, and all the rest worth 4, how much is the group of eggs in the nest worth?

Flower Power

Fill in the numbers on the daisy chain, so that each pair of numbers joined in a straight line adds up to 17.

5

16

15

10

9

6

4   14

Code Crackers

Help the spies unlock the code for a secret safe by fitting all the numbers into the grid. When the puzzle is completed, the numbers in the yellow squares can be used to open the safe.

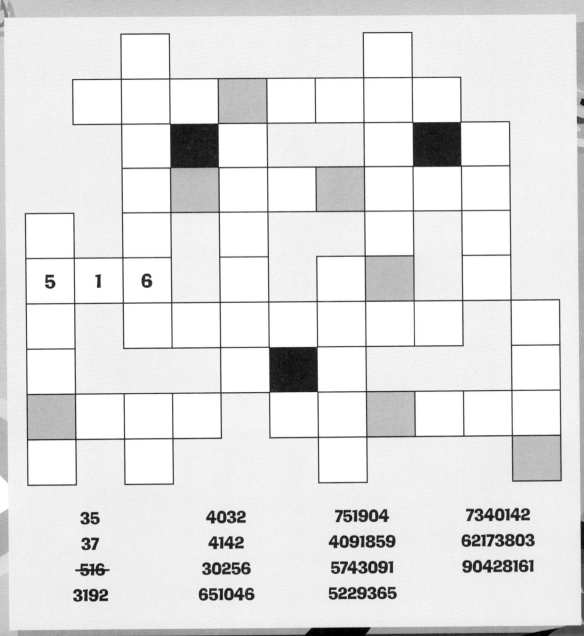

35	4032	751904	7340142
37	4142	4091859	62173803
~~516~~	30256	5743091	90428161
3192	651046	5229365	

Toy Totals

How much is each toy worth? Look at the totals for each row on the right and for each column along the bottom. This will help you work it out. One price is already given.

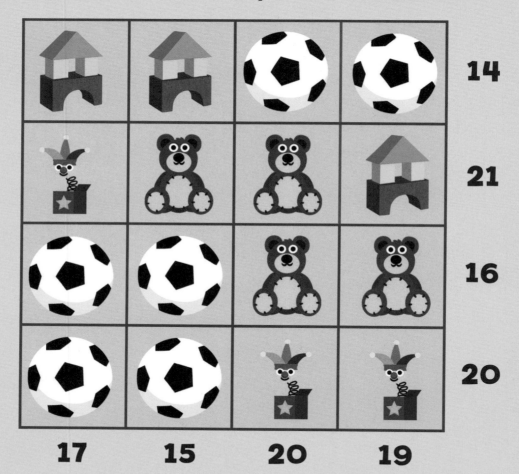

				14
				21
				16
				20
17	**15**	**20**	**19**	

4			

Sweet Treats

Look at the prices of each dessert, then figure out how much each plate of treats is worth. Which one dessert has to be added to plates A to D to make them equal to E?

3	4	5	6	7	8

A

B

C

D

E

Pass to Score

Find a way to get the basketball through the hoop
using the odd numbers only.

Treasure Trail

Starting at the "X", move in the direction on each arrow by that number of squares. So "↑ 3" means move up 3 squares. The directions lead to the buried treasure. Where is it?

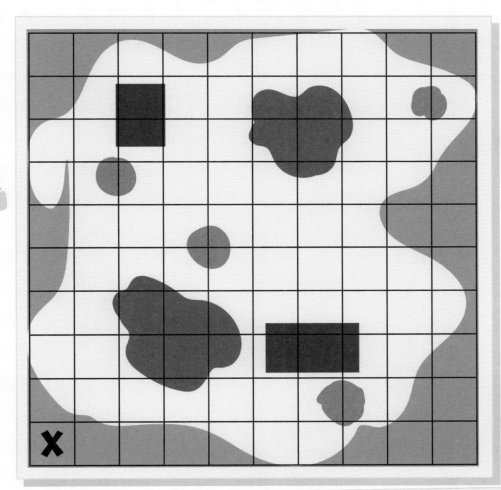

↑3 →5 ↑3 ←2 ↑2 →5 ↓1 ←1 ↓2

←3 ↓2 →1 ↓3 →1 ↑1 →1 ↑2 →1

Farmer's Day

Farmer Joe starts work on the farm at 7:30 in the morning. Look at his list of jobs and the time they take. When does he finish his work?

Feeding the cows	45 minutes
Collecting eggs	15 minutes
Feeding the chickens	20 minutes
Milking the cows	1 hour 20 minutes
Feeding the pigs	40 minutes
Lunch break	1 hour
Repairing a fence	2 hours 15 minutes
Cleaning the cowshed	1 hour 25 minutes
Feeding the sheep	30 minutes

Mountaineers

The number in each square is the sum of the numbers in the two squares below it. Fill in all the empty squares.

13

7

3   2   1

Balloon Burst

Which three balloons should you pop to make the numbers in the remaining balloons add up to 26?

3

5

11

6

10

7

Shopping List

Look at the prices of the fruit and vegetables. How much will this shopping list cost?

5

3

4

2

1

4

5

3

2

3

3

2

7

8

SHOPPING LIST

3 Carrots

1 Cauliflower

3 Tomatoes

2 Broccoli

1 Pumpkin

3 Onions

2 Corn

4 Potatoes

2 Bananas

3 Oranges

3 Pears

6 Strawberries

2 Apples

1 Watermelon

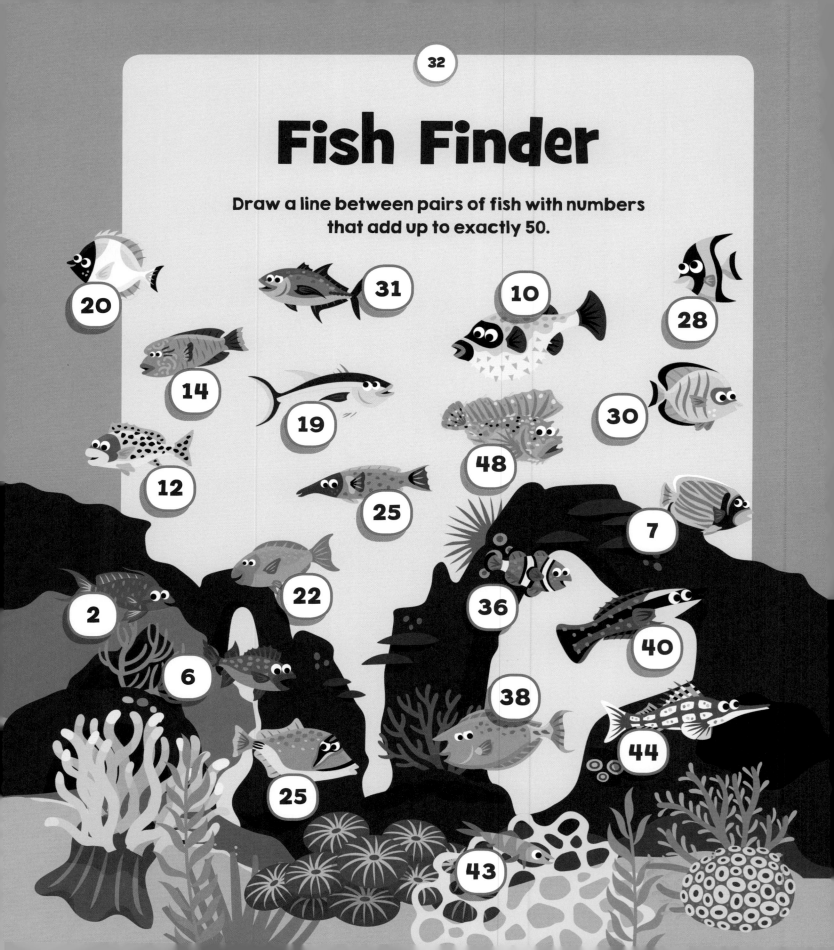

Fish Finder

Draw a line between pairs of fish with numbers that add up to exactly 50.

Busy Baker

The baker has 48 sprinkles for cupcakes, 32 for donuts, and 30 chocolate pieces for cookies. How many should go on each one, so that each different type of treat has the same share?

Bee Buddies

Can you find four bees with numbers that add up to exactly 20 next to each other in a 2 x 2 square?

1	5	3	8	6	1	7	12
11	4	7	3	7	9	4	2
2	6	1	10	3	4	8	13
14	1	13	3	5	9	1	2
2	6	1	9	2	6	3	15
7	9	2	6	4	9	3	1
4	3	6	5	3	7	2	15
8	6	4	8	5	8	1	3

Hidden Art

Shade in the even-numbered squares to reveal a hidden picture.

3	43	89	67	4	7	51	8	9	93	41	73
7	11	12	42	10	34	12	6	14	12	5	1
25	13	52	5	15	91	5	23	9	8	87	5
63	5	2	45	8	17	11	6	31	10	15	91
2	21	38	3	10	83	97	4	87	2	9	8
74	4	96	9	53	69	7	71	11	78	2	10
12	13	8	37	14	8	16	12	3	14	23	6
65	1	4	17	6	13	75	38	1	96	51	9
62	18	12	5	2	52	4	10	27	12	46	4
83	19	16	25	13	29	81	53	7	56	3	5
11	7	10	2	14	46	6	34	4	10	21	63
9	47	27	5	15	2	8	1	7	85	9	49

Wild Weigh-In

Each animal is given a number for its weight. Which one animal is needed to balance each set of scales?

Around the World

**Follow the passengers around the world.
How many passengers are there at the end of
the trip?**

Big Ben:
40 passengers
start the trip.

Eiffel Tower:
2 leave, 10 join
the trip.

**Leaning Tower
of Pisa: 3 leave,
6 join.**

Colosseum:
5 leave, 2 join.

Pyramids:
4 leave, 8 join.

Taj Mahal:
9 leave, 7 join.

Great Wall:
3 leave, 6 join.

**Sydney Opera
House: 11 leave,
2 join.**

Dance Off

All of the dancers won prizes, but who gained the most points overall? Check the prize chart to find out.

1 — 3rd, 2nd, 2nd

2 — 1st, 3rd

3 — 4th, 4th, 1st

4 — 2nd, 3rd, 3rd

5 — 2nd, 1st, 1st

⭐ 1st = 40	⭐ 2nd = 30	⭐ 3rd = 20	⭐ 4th = 10
⭐ 1st = 30	⭐ 2nd = 25	⭐ 3rd = 20	⭐ 4th = 15

⭐ 1st = 20	⭐ 2nd = 10	⭐ 3rd = 5
⭐ 1st = 25	⭐ 2nd = 15	⭐ 3rd = 10

Stepping Stones

Find a path over the stones going up in the three times table.

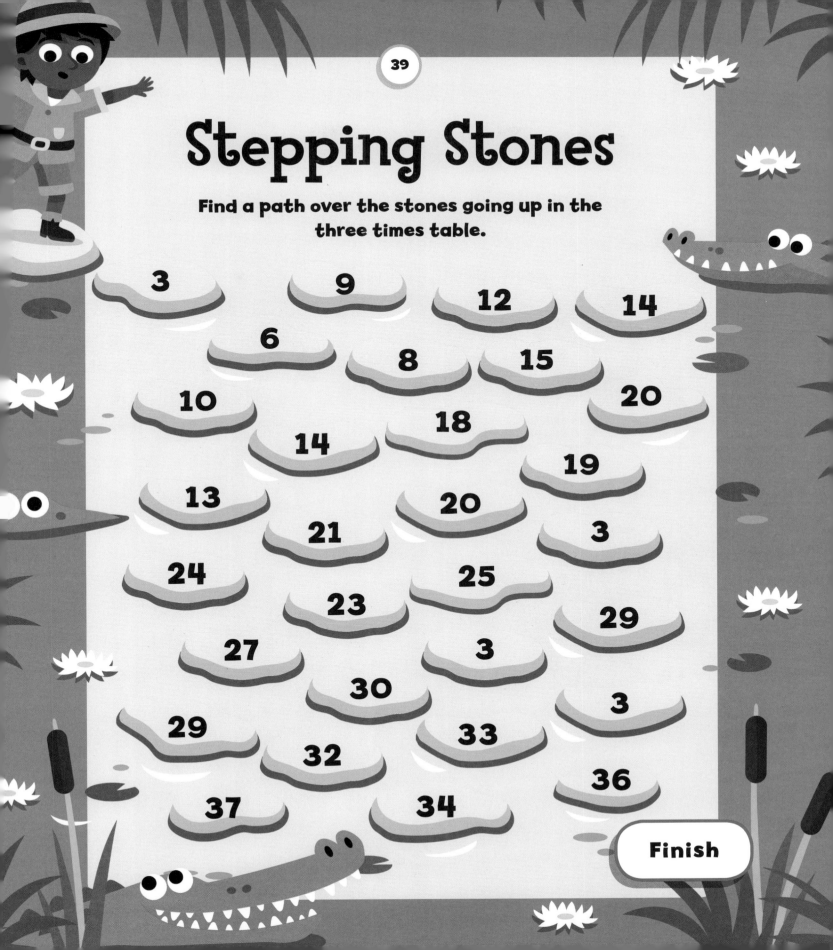

3   9   12   14

6   8   15

10   20

14   18

19

13   20   3

21

24   25

23   29

27   3

30

29   3

33

32

36

37   34

Finish

Penguin Posse

Each ice floe must contain a number of penguins equal to a multiple of 4. How many penguins from each ice floe must jump into the water?

A

B

C

D

Rowing Race

All of these ships sailed 50 miles to reach Athens, but which one got there in the fastest time?

Ship 1

Sailed 20 m.p.h. for 2 hours, then 10 m.p.h. for the rest of the journey.

Ship 2

Sailed 15 m.p.h. for the whole journey.

Ship 3

Sailed 20 miles in 1 hour, 15 miles in the next hour, 10 miles in the next hour, then 5 miles for the next hour.

Ship 4

Sailed 30 m.p.h. for 30 mins, then 20 m.p.h. for 1 hour, then 15 m.p.h. for the rest of the journey.

Ship 5

Sailed 25 miles in 1 hour, 10 miles in the next 45 mins, then 15 miles in the next hour.

Full Bloom

All but one flower in each bunch belongs to a times table.
Circle those flowers.

4 **12** **20** **16** **17** **8**

10 **35** **20** **52** **15** **25**

9 **6** **24** **21** **16** **12**

42 **18** **12** **23** **6** **36**

Reverse Spells

To turn the frogs back into princes, the wizard needs to reverse his spells. Undo all the equations to find out each prince's starting number.

Prince Sven

.... $+ 3 \div 3 \times 2 = 10$

Prince Roger

.... $- 4 \times 4 \div 3 = 8$

Prince Karlos

.... $\div 5 + 3 \times 2 = 16$

Cosmic Cash

These aliens have stopped at a galactic fuel station to buy power cells for their spaceship. Power cells cost 4 astrodollars. The aliens have 100 solar coins and 80 lunar coins. Look at the chart to work out how many cells they can buy.

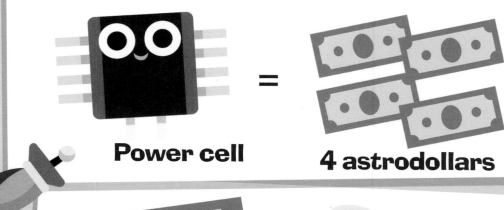

Power cell = **4 astrodollars**

1 astrodollar = **5 solar coins**

1 astrodollar = **20 lunar coins**

Safe Path

Watch your step! The coordinates show where there are mines. Mark them on the grid, then draw a path from A to B. Keep one square in between the mine and the path.

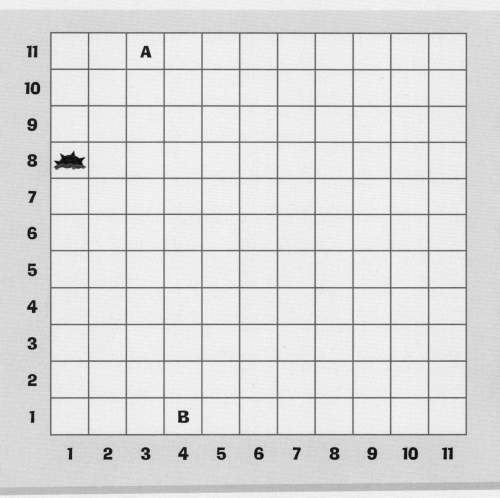

The mines are in these locations.
The first is marked for you:

1, 8; 1 ,10; 3, 3; 3, 7; 5, 7; 5, 11; 6, 2; 7, 6; 9, 2; 9, 8; 9, 9; 11, 4.

Chick Check

Which bird is the chick's parent? Put its number through the equation. If the answer matches the number on the egg, it's the mother!

10

16

30

18

24

28

8

$$? + 4 \div 2 - 5 =$$

36

9

In the Air

Finish the number sequence for each juggler.

A: 17 14 14 .... 20 23 .... (23, 20, 17, 14, ...)

B: 6 10 4 2 .... (2, 4, 6, ...)

C: 32 16 64 128 .... (128, 64, 32, 16, ...)

D: 16 25 9 4 .... (4, 9, 16, 25, ...)

Fruit Picker

Which one fruit in each group needs to be removed to make the numbers on the fruits add up to the large total?

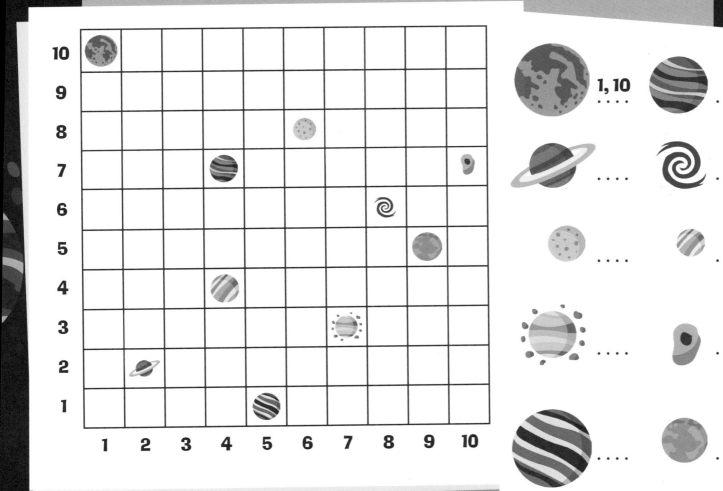

Star Map

Help map the solar system.
Write the coordinates of the planets, moons, and asteroids.

1, 10 . . . .

. . . .

. . . .

. . . .

. . . .

. . . .

Coral Class

**Which group of fish cannot be exactly
divided by 3, 4, or 5?**

Fashion Figures

Who has bought the most expensive set of clothes?

Ella

5
11
13
9

Joseph

15
5
13
6

Mel

9
7
3
18

Sinan

13
10
7
11

Nice Slice

Match the slices of pie with the fractions.

| 1/4 | 1/3 | 2/3 | 1/8 | 1/2 | 3/4 |

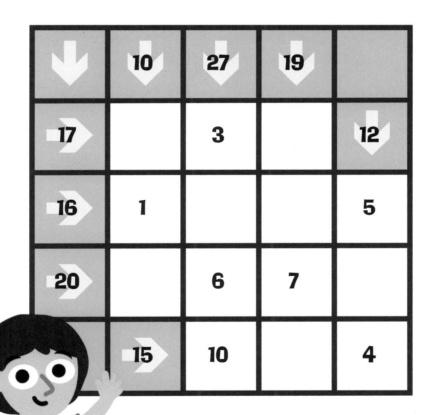

Check Out

Fill the grid with numbers, so that the total for each column and row matches the number on the arrow above and on the left.

Ski Four

Find a route down the mountain, and ski through every number you can divide exactly by 4.

12

13

40

10

8

10

6

14

16

22

18

22

20

24

26

44

32

27

30

36

30

26

30

4

34

38

41

42

48

46

52

46

28

54

50

Brain Bots

Figure out what the robots do to each number,
then fill in their blank answers.

A

3	?	=	9
5	?	=	25
10	?	=	100
6	?	=	......

B

4	?	=	12
6	?	=	18
9	?	=	27
2	?	=	......

C

20	?	=	10
16	?	=	8
14	?	=	7
4	?	=	......

Pups' Picks

Each group of dogs is given 26 chewy bones and 12 tasty bones. If each dog in a group is given the same number of each type of treat, how many will each dog get? Hint: there will be treats left over!

Chewy bones

Tasty bones

Code Clues

Help the detectives crack the code.
What number is represented by each letter?
They have already solved the letter A!

F	E	A	C	B	D

$$A = 6$$
$$B = A \div 2$$
$$C = F + 5$$
$$D = C - F$$
$$E = B^2$$
$$F = A \div B \times 4$$

Marathon Run

Gemma set off on a run at 2:00 p.m., and by 5:30 p.m. she had run 21 miles. If she keeps running at the same speed, how far will she have run by 6:00 p.m. and 7:30 p.m.?

More or Less

Compare the pairs of numbers, decimals, percentages, and fractions. Use the symbols > and < to show which numbers are bigger or smaller.

½	......	60%
50	......	7²
10%	......	1/5
1/100	......	10%
20%	......	1/4
4/5	......	75%
5²	......	50
1/3	......	40%
10.5	......	5.1
50%	......	3/4

Swim Away

Yesterday, there were 16 yellow fish, 15 red fish, and 20 green fish. Count the fish now. Which group has lost the highest percentage?

Number Study

Find a path from the left to the right on connected hexagons, only stepping on odd numbers.

12		12		48		85		22
44	41		79		65		23	
	37	25		92		10		15
13		76	30		21		28	
	64		93	40		75		70
76		52		12	36		46	
	14		67		83	35		60
98		83		71		13	73	
	43		66		74		54	72
42		67	34		53		89	
	86		21		94	62		12
53		82	33		55		44	

Train Trip

A passenger has to take five trains to get to the airport. If she catches the first at 10:00 a.m., when does she arrive at the airport?

1 Journey time: 1 hour, 50 minutes.

2 Leaves 15 minutes later.

Journey time: 40 minutes.

3 Leaves 30 minutes later.

Journey time: 1 hour, 10 mins.

4 Leaves 10 minutes later.

Journey time: 40 minutes.

5 Leaves 20 minutes later.

Arrives at airport 25 minutes later.

Cycle Track

This map shows how many minutes it takes to cycle between different points. What is the shortest journey:
from A to B; from B to C; from C to D; from A to D?

A 13 10 3 7
7 5 8
13 4 B 4
15 3 6
13 12 4
15 3
11 C 9 6
8 5
6 15
3 7 4 D

Magic Match

The fairy godmother is using equation spells.
Which equations give the same results?

3 x 4

9 x 3

24 ÷ 4

6 x 2

2 x 9

18 ÷ 3

100 ÷ 4

3 x 6

5 x 5

30 ÷ 2

30 - 3

5 x 3

Square Pairs

This robot loves square numbers. Match the numbers with their squares.

3

8

36

6

64

81

100

9

4

5

16

7

10

25

49

Adding Animals

Complete the grid with numbers from 1 to 9, so that they add up to the total on the arrow pointing to the row or column. No numbers can be repeated in a row or column.

Shoe Store

Shoes with numbers that can be exactly divided by 3, 4, or 5 have been sold. Which shoes are still for sale?

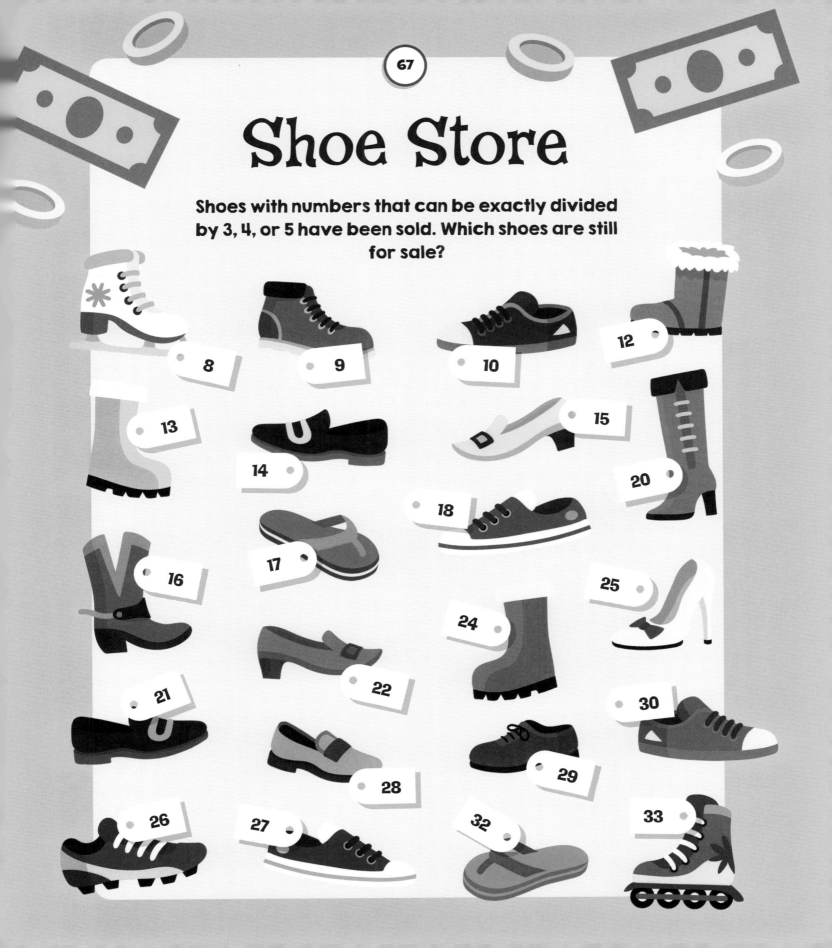

Cake Count

Belinda baked a different number of treats. The tray shows the total amounts for each kind. Look at how many her friends bought. How many of each kind does Belinda have left?

Belinda baked:

24 ....

20 ....

22 ....

18 ....

36 ....

30 ....

Manuel bought:

4 6 6 2 2

Julia bought:

4 3 5 2 10

Maxine bought:

4 3 8 12

Sam bought:

3 5 6 5 4 8

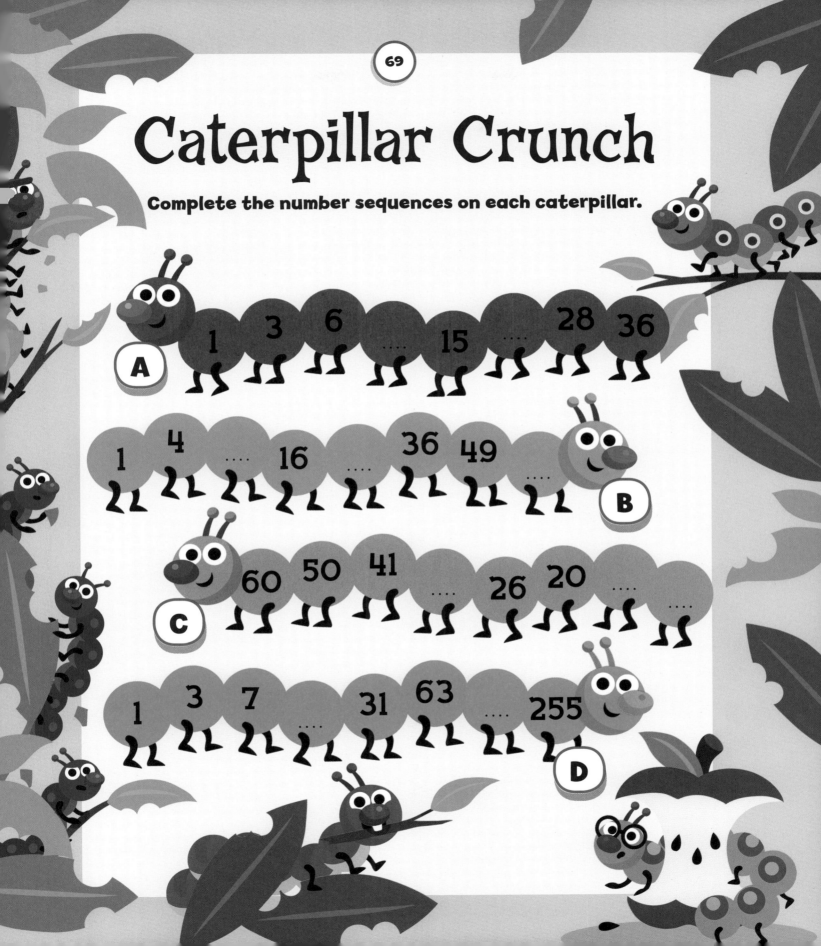

Caterpillar Crunch

Complete the number sequences on each caterpillar.

A 1 3 6 .... 15 .... 28 36

B 1 4 .... 16 .... 36 49

C 60 50 41 .... 26 20 ....

D 1 3 7 .... 31 63 255

Blowing Bubbles

Jim is blowing bubbles to match the 3 times table; Susie is matching the 4 times table. Which three bubbles belong in both times tables? Which three bubbles do not belong in either times table?

15 6 39 16 36

3 40 12 21 28 18

33 22 30 8

10 32

24 20

27 38

9 4

Tricky Trolls

Naughty trolls have covered up the symbols in the equations. Figure out what they should be by looking at the numbers.

A $3 \; ? \; 4 \; ? \; 2 = 10$

B $20 \; ? \; 4 \; ? \; 6 = 11$

C $32 \; ? \; 8 \; ? \; 3 = 8$

D $7 \; ? \; 4 \; ? \; 5 = 33$

E $17 \; ? \; 3 \; ? \; 4 = 5$

Royal Share

The king is giving away his riches. Divide the different coins and gems equally between the four princes. How many of each do they get?

....

....

....

....

Run and Jump

Who came 1st, 2nd, and 3rd in the hurdles race? Check the runners' times in the chart, and add five seconds for every hurdle they hit.

Runner	Finish Time	Hurdles Hit	Total Time	Finishing Place
1	40 seconds	3		
2	52 seconds	2		
3	36 seconds	4		
4	48 seconds	1		

Cool Cookies

**Becky's been baking cookies.
Which cookie shapes only have one line
of symmetry? Ignore the sprinkles!**

Mug Shot

Help the police track a criminal. Shade the
squares in the grid with numbers from the 4 times
table to reveal the bad guy's face.

44	12	20	16	28	8	6	17	22	14	40	24
8	46	24	12	38	30	26	14	40	12	42	16
12	22	25	15	9	14	34	8	10	26	30	8
24	46	44	16	12	46	26	16	24	12	34	12
41	24	30	28	31	22	6	13	12	10	4	35
28	34	2	18	27	31	15	26	30	9	21	16
18	23	22	33	44	14	22	8	34	18	30	22
12	14	19	30	31	20	32	21	18	10	14	24
40	44	46	30	22	13	15	34	38	42	36	28
24	4	26	36	8	12	32	36	40	39	20	16
36	12	18	32	30	28	23	26	32	33	16	4
4	28	34	21	44	32	28	12	6	18	12	8

Balancing Act

Look at the balanced scales to work out how much all the toys weigh, then complete the weight chart.

🦆	🦖	🧸	🃏	🏀	🤖
2					

Cross Over

Starting at the number 3, plan a route over the bridges, following the equations as you go. Which route leads you to the number 27?

Tricky Timetable

If you leave at 8:00 a.m., which trains, ferries, and planes should you catch to get from A to D to arrive before 3:00 p.m.?

TRAVEL INFORMATION			
Time	Type	Travel from	Time taken
8:00 a.m.	Train	A to B	4 hours
8:30 a.m.	Train	A to B	3 hours
9:10 a.m.	Ferry	A to B	2¾ hours
11:00 a.m.	Ferry	B to C	2 hours
11:15 a.m.	Train	B to C	2½ hours
11:45 a.m.	Plane	A to C	2½ hours
11:45 a.m.	Train	B to C	1½ hours
12:00 p.m.	Ferry	B to C	1 hour
12:30 p.m.	Train	C to D	2 hours
1:00 p.m.	Ferry	C to D	1½ hours
1:15 p.m.	Train	C to D	1¼ hours
1:55 p.m.	Plane	C to D	1¼ hours
2:30 p.m.	Train	C to D	1 hour

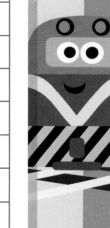

Sports Scores

The sports results are shown as mathemathical problems, but one result for each sport is different from the rest. Which results are the odd ones out?

1

TENNIS SCORES

7 x 4 = ...

13 + 15 = ...

0 - 2 = ...

6 x 5 = ...

14 x 2 = ...

2

SOCCER SCORES

80 ÷ 2 = ...

7 x 6 = ...

25 + 15 = ...

4 x 10 = ...

8 x 5 = ...

3

GOLF SCORES

3 x 6 = ...

30 - 12 = ...

2 x 9 = ...

11 x 7 = ...

4 x 4 = ...

4

BASKETBALL SCORES

8 x 3 = ...

4 x 6 = ...

8 + 14 = ...

48 ÷ 2 = ...

30 - 6 = ...

Gnome Homes

Three gnomes can live in each toadstool.
If there are 27 gnomes and 16 toadstools,
how many more gnomes can fit in the
toadstools?

Candy Count

What is the percentage of red, yellow, and purple jelly beans in this collection?

Solutions

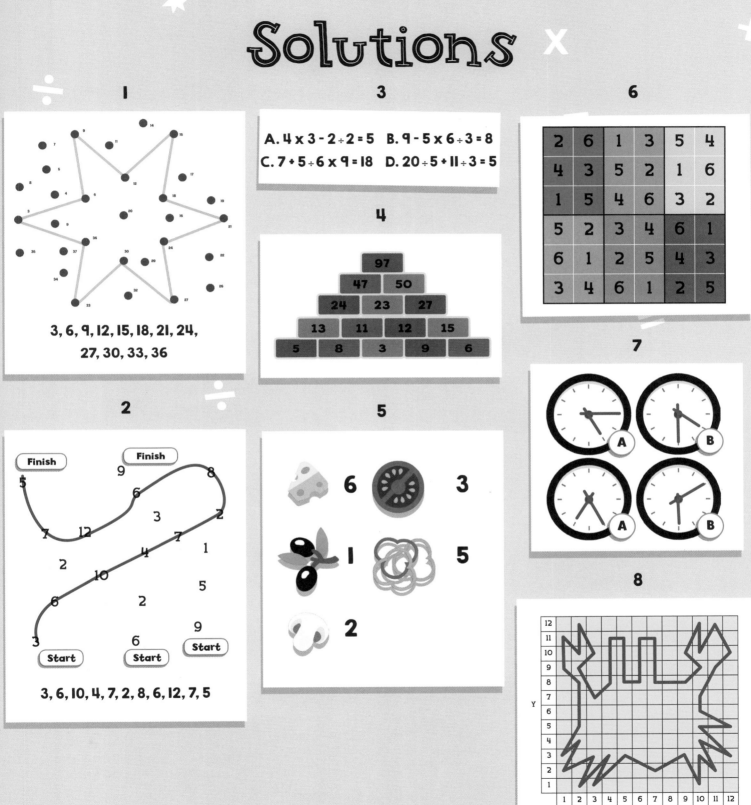

1

3, 6, 9, 12, 15, 18, 21, 24, 27, 30, 33, 36

2

3, 6, 10, 4, 7, 2, 8, 6, 12, 7, 5

3

A. 4 x 3 - 2 ÷ 2 = 5   B. 9 - 5 x 6 ÷ 3 = 8
C. 7 + 5 ÷ 6 x 9 = 18   D. 20 ÷ 5 + 11 ÷ 3 = 5

4

97
47 50
24 23 27
13 11 12 15
5 8 3 9 6

5

6   3   1   5   2

6

2	6	1	3	5	4
4	3	5	2	1	6
1	5	4	6	3	2
5	2	3	4	6	1
6	1	2	5	4	3
3	4	6	1	2	5

7

8

Solutions

9

The hamster won the most!

Poodle = 40

Terrier = 35

Rabbit = 45

Cat = 55

Budgie = 45

Hamster = 60

11

	x 2	+ 4	x 3	- 7
10	20	14	30	3
7	14	11	21	0
12	24	16	36	5
20	40	24	60	13

15

10

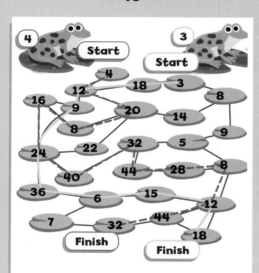

Frog 4: 4, 12, 20, 8, 16, 24, 40, 32, 44, 28, 8, 12, 48, 32.

Frog 3: 3, 18, 12, 9, 24, 36, 6, 15, 12, 18.

12

Angela got the farthest: number 33

13

Archer A scored 32,
Archer B scored 38,
Archer C scored 27,
so Archer B wins!

14

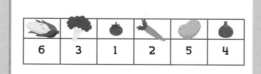					
6	3	1	2	5	4

Corn 6, Broccoli 3, Tomato 1, Carrot 2, Potato 5, Onion 4.

16

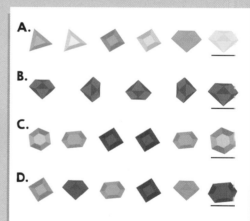

A. Order is blue, yellow 3-sided gem, blue, yellow 4-sided gem, blue, yellow 5-sided gem.

B. Order is pink gem making a quarter turn each time.

C. Order is 6-sided yellow gem, 6-sided green gem, 4-sided red gem, then the same backward.

D. Order is green, red, green, red, repeated, with 4-sided, 5-sided and 6-sided gems, and repeat.

Solutions

17

5 have spots, 5 stripes
and 5 stars, leaving
5 without patterns.

18

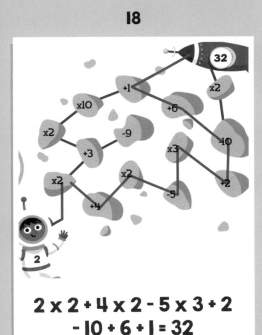

$$2 \times 2 + 4 \times 2 - 5 \times 3 + 2 - 10 + 6 + 1 = 32$$

19

TRAIN Home Town to Midvale
10, BUS Midvale to Breezy
Beach 12, and CAR Breezy
Beach to Cheap City 19 = 41.

20

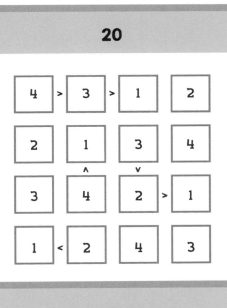

21

The value of the eggs
in the nest equals 80.

22

23

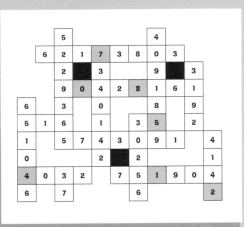

Solutions

24

🏠	🧸	🎪	⚽
4	5	7	3

25

Plate A: 5

Plate B: 8

Plate C: 6

Plate D: 5

26

13 10 26 23 3 14 19 11 4 16 5 33 9 21 15 18 9 17 7 8 1

27

28

4:00 in the afternoon.

29

46

25 21

12 13 8

5 7 6 2

3 2 5 1 1

30

3 11 5 6 7 10

Solutions

31

The shopping will cost 108.

32

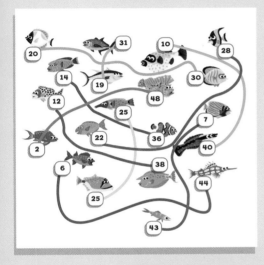

33

The baker adds 8 sprinkles to each cupcake, 8 to each donut, and 5 chocolate pieces to each cookie.

34

1	5	3	8	6	1	7	12
11	4	7	3	7	9	4	2
2	6	1	10	3	4	8	13
14	1	13	3	5	9	1	2
2	6	1	9	2	6	3	15
7	9	2	6	4	9	3	1
4	3	6	5	3	5	7	15
8	6	4	8	5	8	1	3

35

3	43	89	67	4	7	51	8	9	93	41	73
7	11	12	42	10	34	12	6	14	12	5	1
25	13	52	5	15	91	5	23	9	8	87	5
63	5	2	45	8	17	11	6	31	10	15	91
2	21	38	3	10	83	97	4	87	2	9	8
74	4	96	9	53	69	7	71	11	78	2	10
12	13	8	37	14	8	16	12	3	14	23	6
65	1	4	17	6	13	75	38	1	96	51	9
62	18	12	5	2	52	4	10	27	12	46	4
83	19	16	25	13	29	81	53	7	56	3	5
11	7	10	2	14	46	16	34	4	10	21	63
9	47	27	5	15	2	8	1	7	85	9	49

36

Scale 1: Koala (4)
Scale 2: Warthog (6)
Scale 3: Zebra (12)
Scale 4: Ostrich (7).

37

44

38

Dancer 1 won 55,
Dancer 2 won 50,
Dancer 3 won 50,
Dancer 4 won 55,
Dancer 5 won 65,
so Dancer 5 gained the most points overall.

Solutions

39

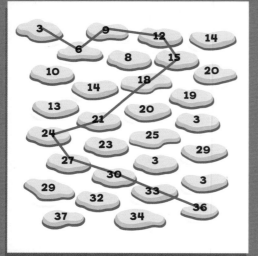

40

Group A: 3
Group B: 3
Group C: 2
Group D: 2

41

Ship 1 took 3 hours.

Ship 2 took 3 hours and 20 minutes.

Ship 3 took 4 hours.

Ship 4 took 2 hours and 30 minutes.

Ship 5 took 2 hours and 45 minutes.

So, Ship 4 was the fastest.

42

43

Prince Sven = 12,
Prince Roger = 10,
Prince Karlos = 25.

44

100 solar coins = 20 astrodollars.
80 lunar coins = 4 astrodollars.
So, the aliens can buy
6 power cells.

Solutions

45

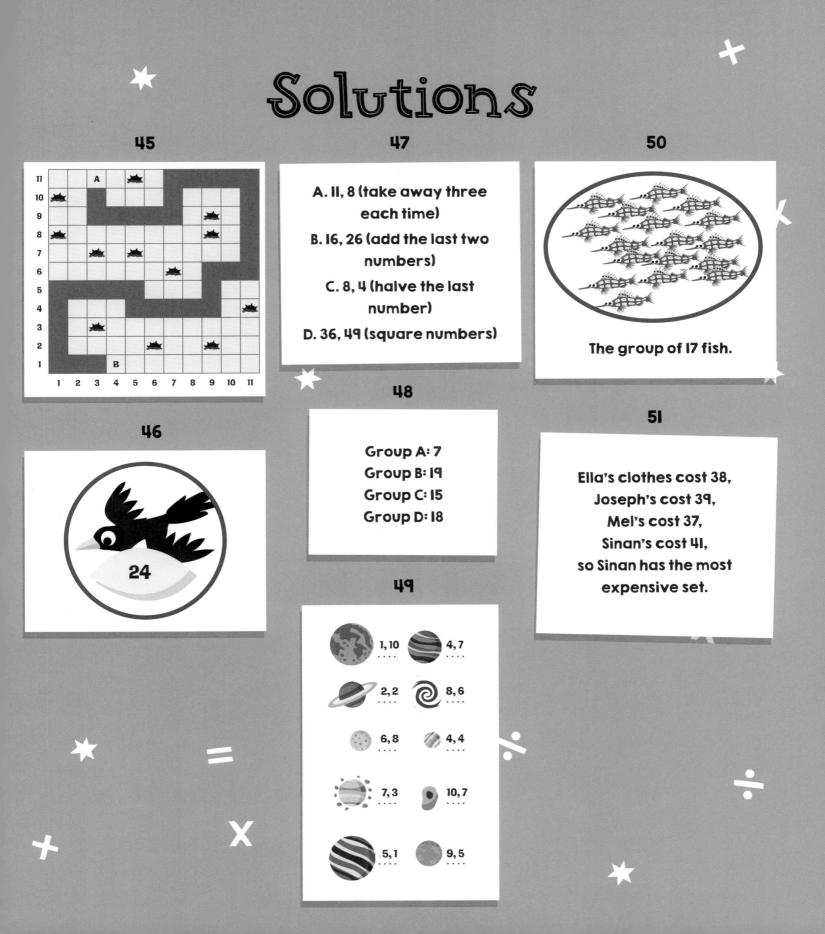

47

A. 11, 8 (take away three each time)

B. 16, 26 (add the last two numbers)

C. 8, 4 (halve the last number)

D. 36, 49 (square numbers)

50

The group of 17 fish.

46

24

48

Group A: 7
Group B: 19
Group C: 15
Group D: 18

51

Ella's clothes cost 38,
Joseph's cost 39,
Mel's cost 37,
Sinan's cost 41,
so Sinan has the most expensive set.

49

1, 10

4, 7

2, 2

8, 6

6, 8

4, 4

7, 3

10, 7

5, 1

9, 5

Solutions

52

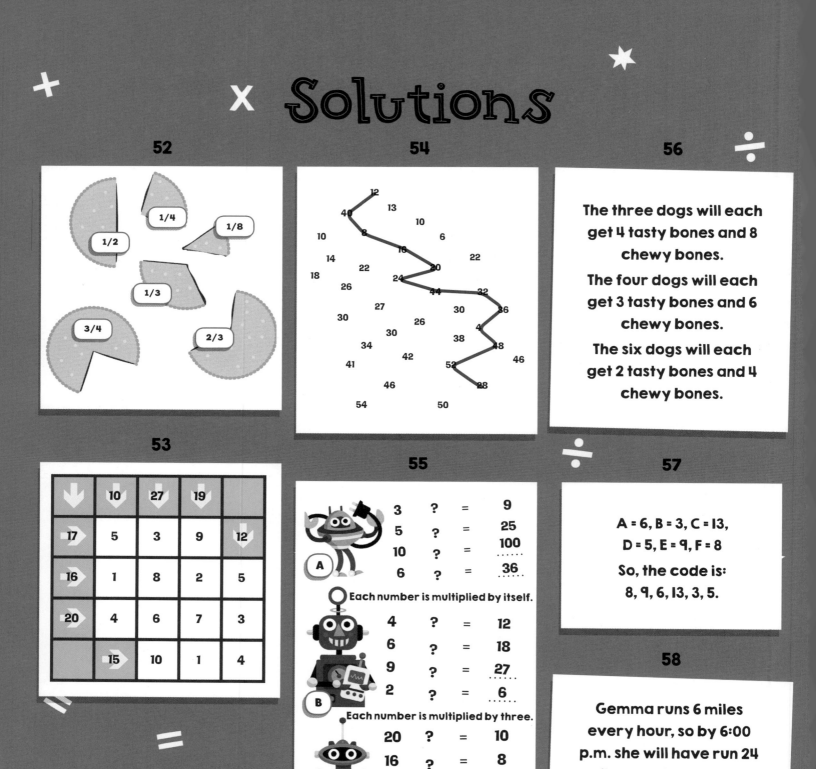

1/4
1/8
1/2
1/3
3/4
2/3

53

⬇	10	27	19	
17 ➡	5	3	9	12 ⬇
16 ➡	1	8	2	5
20 ➡	4	6	7	3
	15 ➡	10	1	4

54

12
13
40
10
8
10
6
10
16
22
14
22
20
18
26
24
44
32
30
27
30
36
34
26
4
30
38
48
41
42
52
46
46
28
54
50

55

3	?	=	9
5	?	=	25
10	?	=	100
6	?	=	36

A

Each number is multiplied by itself.

4	?	=	12
6	?	=	18
9	?	=	27
2	?	=	6

B

Each number is multiplied by three.

20	?	=	10
16	?	=	8
14	?	=	7
4	?	=	2

C

Each number is divided by 2.

56

The three dogs will each get 4 tasty bones and 8 chewy bones.

The four dogs will each get 3 tasty bones and 6 chewy bones.

The six dogs will each get 2 tasty bones and 4 chewy bones.

57

A = 6, B = 3, C = 13, D = 5, E = 9, F = 8

So, the code is: 8, 9, 6, 13, 3, 5.

58

Gemma runs 6 miles every hour, so by 6:00 p.m. she will have run 24 miles, and by 7:30 p.m. she will have run 33 miles.

Solutions

59

1/2 < 60%.

50 > 7^2

10% < 1/5

1/100 < 10%.

20% < 1/4

4/5 > 75%.

5^2 < 50

1/3 < 40%.

10.5 > 5.1

50% < 3/4

60

There are 8 yellow fish, 10 red, and 12 green, so the yellow fish lost 50%., the red lost 33.33%., and the green lost 40%.. The yellow fish lost the highest percentage.

61

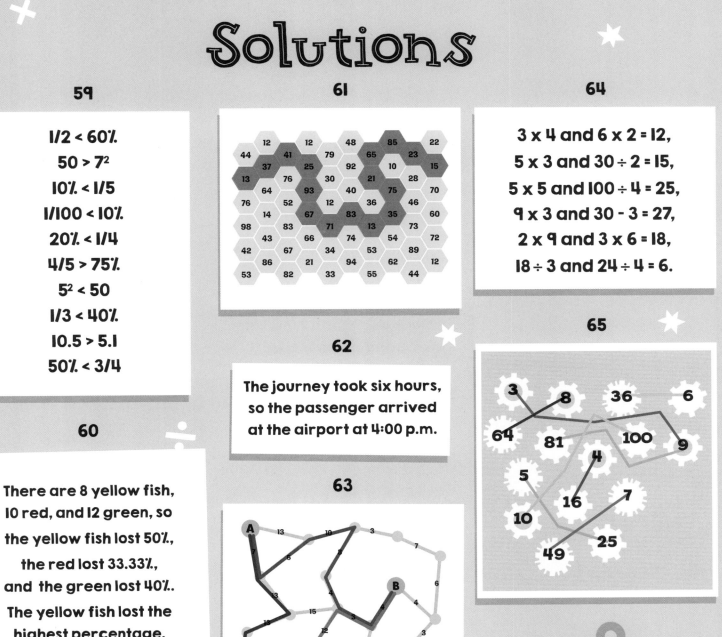

62

The journey took six hours, so the passenger arrived at the airport at 4:00 p.m.

63

64

3 x 4 and 6 x 2 = 12,

5 x 3 and 30 ÷ 2 = 15,

5 x 5 and 100 ÷ 4 = 25,

9 x 3 and 30 - 3 = 27,

2 x 9 and 3 x 6 = 18,

18 ÷ 3 and 24 ÷ 4 = 6.

65

Solutions

66

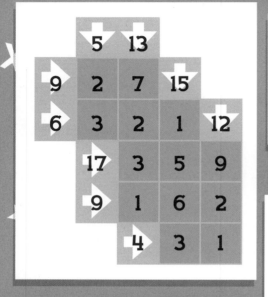

67

68

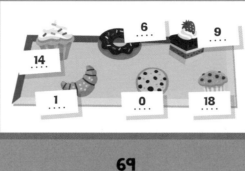

69

Caterpillar A (add 2, then 3, then 4, and so on): 1, 3, 6, 10, 15, 21, 28, 36.

B (square numbers): 1, 4, 9, 16, 25, 36, 49, 64.

C (subtract 10, then 9, then 8, and so on): 60, 50, 41, 33, 26, 20, 15, 11.

D (double + 1): 1, 3, 7, 15, 31, 63, 127, 255.

70

12, 24, and 36 belong in both 3 and 4 times tables. 10, 22, and 38 do not belong in either times tables.

71

A. 3 x 4 - 2 = 10
B. 20 ÷ 4 + 6 = 11
C. 32 - 8 ÷ 3 = 8
D. 7 x 4 + 5 = 33
E. 17 + 3 ÷ 4 = 5

72

Each prince gets 6 gold coins, 9 silver coins, 5 blue gems, and 7 red gems.